Original title:
Cozy Reflections on a Winter Night

Copyright © 2024 Creative Arts Management OÜ
All rights reserved.

Author: Sebastian Whitmore
ISBN HARDBACK: 978-9916-94-412-7
ISBN PAPERBACK: 978-9916-94-413-4

Lanterns of Peace in the Stillness

In the night, lanterns glow bright,
Casting shadows, soothing the fright.
Whispers of calm dance in the air,
Unity wrapped in gentle care.

Stars shimmer like wishes untold,
Stories of peace begin to unfold.
Hearts entwined in a soft embrace,
Finding solace in this sacred space.

Soft Echoes of Comfort in the Cold

Winter winds hum a soft lullaby,
Echoes of warmth as the snowflakes fly.
Inviting us close, where hearts align,
In the chill, love's light does shine.

Fireside flickers, a dance of gold,
Reminders of comfort against the cold.
We gather near, sharing soft glances,
Finding joy in these quiet romances.

Sipping Warmth from the Heart

A cup in hand, steam rises high,
Sipping warmth as moments fly by.
Each drop a treasure, rich and dear,
Bringing forth laughter, wiping each tear.

Invited to pause, we savor the blend,
In every sip, love's message we send.
Echoes of friendship, sweet and refined,
Sipping warmth, two souls intertwined.

Beneath the Blanket of a Silver Moon

The night wraps softly in silver light,
Dreams whisper secrets, taking flight.
Beneath the moon, shadows retreat,
In its embrace, the world feels complete.

Stars twinkle like memories shared,
A canvas of hope, gently declared.
In the hush of the night, we find our tune,
Safe and sound beneath the moon.

Twilight Embraced by Snowflakes

As twilight falls with gentle grace,
Snowflakes waltz in a soft embrace.
Each flake unique, a fleeting art,
Whispers of peace that warm the heart.

The world transformed, a silver hue,
Blankets of white, a dream anew.
Footsteps muffled, a silent song,
In winter's arms, where we belong.

Stars peek through the evening light,
Guiding us through the winter night.
Fires crackle, shadows dance,
In this stillness, we take a chance.

Twilight's beauty, a fleeting glow,
Wrapped in warmth, where love can grow.
As snowflakes fall, our spirits rise,
In winter's grasp, we touch the skies.

Winter's Echoes in a Familiar Room

In a familiar room where silence reigns,
Winter's whispers touch the panes.
Frosted glass, a crystal scene,
Memories linger, soft and serene.

The clock ticks slow, its hands embrace,
Moments captured, time's gentle trace.
Old photographs in dusty frames,
Echoes of laughter, soft refrains.

The fire crackles, warmth aglow,
As winter nights invite the snow.
Each breath a mist, hanging around,
In this haven, peace is found.

As shadows stretch 'neath pale moonlight,
The world outside is pure delight.
In winter's hold, our hearts align,
In this familiar love, we shine.

Popcorn, Giggles, and Snowy Trails

Popcorn pops with joy and cheer,
Laughter echoing far and near.
Snowflakes dance in twilight's glow,
Childish giggles, soft and slow.

Trails of white beneath our feet,
Every step, a joyful beat.
Warm cocoa in our tiny hands,
Wonders shared in winter's lands.

Warm Hearts Amidst Winter's Chill

Winter frost wraps all around,
Yet our dreams refuse to drown.
With each breath, a warmth we share,
Love ignites the cold night air.

Candles flicker in the night,
Holding hands, we feel the light.
Every heartbeat tells a tale,
Together we'll forever sail.

Chilled Air, Warm Hearts

Chilled air whispers through the trees,
A gentle touch, a loving breeze.
In every corner, warmth resides,
Embraced by love, our hearts confide.

Fires flicker, shadows dance,
In this moment, we take a chance.
In frozen nights, our spirits soar,
With memories made, we will explore.

Evening Comforts and Silver Dreams

Evening falls with a soft embrace,
Blankets wrapped in a cozy space.
Silver dreams upon the night,
Guiding souls in gentle flight.

A quiet hum, the world's asleep,
In this solace, love runs deep.
Stars above like eyes that gleam,
In the dark, we chase our dream.

Ember Glow Beneath the Stars

In the stillness of the night,
Embers dance in soft delight.
Whispers rise with every spark,
Painting dreams, igniting dark.

Beneath the vast, celestial dome,
We find our hearts, we find our home.
Sparks of hope in twilight's clasp,
Where silent wishes gently grasp.

Stars above like watchful eyes,
Guide us through the velvet skies.
Their glow reflects in lovers' gaze,
Forever lost in cosmic haze.

Together, in this gentle air,
We cherish moments, light as prayer.
Hand in hand, we journey slow,
In the ember glow, beneath the snow.

Warmth in the Chill

In the crisp of winter's breath,
Fires keep at bay the death.
We gather close, a circle tight,
As shadows dance in flickering light.

Each laugh, each story shared tonight,
Brings warmth to hearts, ignites the bright.
Outside the world may freeze and sway,
But inside love will find its way.

Cocoa steams in mugs we hold,
A simple comfort, rich and bold.
As winds howl like a distant call,
We find our peace, we have it all.

So let the chill embrace the trees,
For we are wrapped in memories.
Together, warmth which never fades,
In laughter's light, the cold dismayed.

Frost-Kissed Dreams

Morning light on frosted leaves,
Nature shimmers, weaves and cleaves.
Each breath a cloud in frozen air,
Whispered hopes float everywhere.

Dreams entwined in icy lace,
Dance across the winter's face.
Memories wrapped in silver glow,
From nights where starlit wishes flow.

We chase the echoes of our past,
Frost-kissed moments meant to last.
Through the chill, our hearts ignite,
In the beauty of silent night.

The world may seem like crystal glass,
But through the cold, we will surpass.
With each dream, we bravely tread,
In the warmth of thoughts we've bred.

The Hushed Lullaby of Night

When nightfall drapes its velvet shroud,
The world grows still, beneath the cloud.
Moonlight sings a gentle tune,
A lullaby for stars and moon.

Crickets chirp in soft refrain,
While shadows dance on windowpane.
Whispers of the breeze take flight,
Carrying dreams on wings of night.

In the quiet, hearts align,
Bathed in silver, sweet divine.
The world may slumber, safe and sound,
In the hush, true peace is found.

Hold this moment close and dear,
As the gentle night draws near.
In its arms, our worries cease,
Wrapped in night's soft, tender peace.

Nightfall's Serenade in a Frosted World

The stars awaken, gleaming bright,
A silvery hush drapes the night.
Frosty whispers dance on the breeze,
Nature's symphony begins to freeze.

Moonlight kisses the silent trees,
Casting shadows, where time agrees.
In this realm, dreams softly twirl,
Nightfall's serenade in a frosted world.

Wrapped in the Embrace of Serenity

Gentle waves caress the shore,
Whispers of peace, forevermore.
Wrapped in the heart of tranquil nights,
Where the spirit soars, and the soul ignites.

Stars twinkle softly in the sky,
As lullabies of the moon draw nigh.
Wrapped in warmth, shadows dissolve,
In the embrace of serenity, we evolve.

The Scent of Pine and Flickering Light

Amidst the woods, a gentle glow,
The scent of pine begins to flow.
Flickering lights in cozy nooks,
Whispering tales like cherished books.

Breezes murmur through the tall trees,
Nature's perfume brings sweet release.
In this haven, time gently sways,
The scent of pine in the golden rays.

Serene Journeys Through the Hazy Night

The moonlit path invites the wanderer,
Through hazy dreams where thoughts can stir.
Each step unfolds the night's embrace,
A serene journey, a tranquil space.

Whispers of night become the song,
Guiding souls to where they belong.
In the stillness, mysteries ignite,
As we travel through the hazy night.

Sipping Cocoa by Candlelight

Warmth in my hands, a cup so sweet,
Flickering flames, a gentle beat.
Whispers of comfort in the air,
Moments like these, beyond compare.

Marshmallows bob, a snowy dream,
Softly we smile, lost in the theme.
Cocoa flows rich, the night is near,
Hearts intertwined, with loved ones here.

Shadows Dance on Frosted Glass

Evening falls, a chill sets in,
Shadows play where light has been.
Frosted panes in quiet grace,
Nature's art, a soft embrace.

Whispers echo, secrets told,
Glimmers of warmth, hearts unfold.
Outside, the world is still and bright,
Inside, we bask in love's warm light.

A Blanket of Stillness

Snowflakes fall, a soft caress,
Blankets snug, we find our rest.
Nature sleeps, in white attire,
The world is hushed, about the fire.

Gentle dreams begin to weave,
In this peace, we dare believe.
Together here, our worries fade,
In this haven, hearts are laid.

The Silence Wrapped in Flannel

Flannel shirts and cozy nights,
Wrapped in warmth, the world feels right.
Silence hums a soothing tune,
Beneath the watchful, watchful moon.

Stars above twinkle in glee,
In this stillness, I am free.
The world outside drifts far away,
In your arms, forever stay.

The Stillness of Time in the Evening Glow

The sun dips low, a golden hue,
Soft whispers of dusk begin to brew.
Shadows stretch, as day takes flight,
In stillness, we hold the night.

Crickets serenade the silent air,
As stars awaken, bright and rare.
Moments weave a tapestry,
In this calm, we find unity.

Cherished Moments in the Cold Embrace

Winter's breath paints the world white,
Frost-kissed branches shiver in twilight.
Each breath a cloud, each step a song,
In this cold, we find where we belong.

Laughter dances on flakes of snow,
Memories wrapped in warmth's soft glow.
With each moment, hearts entwined,
In cherished memories, love defined.

The Glow of Togetherness in the Frost.

Fires crackle, casting shadows tall,
In the hearth's warmth, we hear the call.
Bundled close, we share our dreams,
In frosty air, our laughter beams.

Snowflakes twirl, a magical flight,
Together we shine, our hearts alight.
In the chill, our spirits soar,
In love's embrace, we need no more.

Whispers of Soft Snowfall

As night descends, the world turns hushed,
Snowflakes fall, in silence brushed.
Each flake a whisper, gentle and slow,
Caressing the earth, a pure white glow.

Under the cover of winter's quilt,
Our hearts remember, the warmth we built.
In stillness, we listen, as time drifts away,
In the whispers of snow, forever we'll stay.

Moonlight on Quiet Streets

The silver light drapes softly,
Over cobblestones so bare.
Whispers of the night echo,
In the cool and tender air.

Shadows dance along the walls,
Underneath the starry skies.
Silence fills the empty space,
Where the heart remembers sighs.

Streetlamps flicker with a glow,
Guiding footsteps that remain.
Each corner holds a secret,
Of laughter, joy, and pain.

Moonlight bathes the silent town,
As dreams awaken from their sleep.
In this world of quiet grace,
All the past we wish to keep.

Flickering Flames and Gentle Thoughts

The fire crackles in delight,
Casting shadows on the wall.
Each spark a whisper of the night,
As moments dance and softly fall.

Gentle thoughts float through the air,
Like embers rising, free and light.
In this haven, without care,
We find solace in the night.

Memories wrapped in warmth abound,
Stories shared with smiles and cheer.
In the glow, our hearts are found,
Flickering flames, forever near.

Together in this sacred space,
We embrace the calm and glow.
With each flame, a warm embrace,
And gentle thoughts, like rivers flow.

Tucked Away in Winter's Embrace

Snowflakes whisper as they fall,
Blanketing the earth in white.
Nature rests, so peaceful, small,
In the quiet heart of night.

Frosty breath against the glass,
A world transformed, so still, so pure.
Time seems to slow, a gentle pass,
Winter's touch, both strong and sure.

Families gather, warmth in sight,
Hot cocoa shared with laughter's ring.
In cozy nooks, we find delight,
As the winter winds softly sing.

Tucked away from the cold's embrace,
We cherish moments, soft and bright.
In this space, we find our place,
Winter's magic in the night.

Nighttime Musings beside the Hearth

The hearth glows with a gentle fire,
As thoughts unwind and freely roam.
In the warmth, our hearts conspire,
Creating dreams that feel like home.

Moonlight spills through window panes,
Caressing faces lost in thought.
Outside, a world where silence reigns,
Inside, the solace we have sought.

Softly spoken words ignite,
Reflections in the gentle light.
Embraced in comfort, calm, and bright,
Our souls take flight into the night.

With each crackle, stories told,
We gather close, no need for haste.
In this moment, love unfolds,
Nighttime musings we embrace.

Whispers of Warmth Beneath the Stars

In the hush of night, we seek,
Silence dances, hearts entwined.
Stars above, a gentle peek,
Moonlight whispers, love defined.

Wrapped in a soft embrace,
Time stands still, moments bloom.
In your eyes, I find my place,
Together, chasing shadows' loom.

Dreams float like feathers light,
Underneath this vast expanse.
In the stillness, pure delight,
Lost in our eternal dance.

Every secret softly shared,
Softly glows in twilight's hue.
With every glance, I am bared,
Whispers of warmth, me and you.

Frost-Kissed Dreams in Twilight Hues

Amidst the chill of vibrant skies,
Frosted breath adorns the trees.
Where every sigh, a soft reprise,
In twilight's hush, the heart agrees.

Dreams linger on a silver thread,
Wrapped in blankets, spirits soar.
Each whisper soft, where love has led,
Beyond the window, flakes implore.

Jewel-like glimmers in the night,
Crystals dance upon the ground.
In this beauty, pure and bright,
Frost-kissed dreams, forever found.

Through every flake, a wish takes flight,
A quiet promise, strong and true.
In this stillness, pure delight,
Frost-kissed dreams, me and you.

Embracing the Silence of a Snowy Eve

Snowflakes drift, a gentle hush,
Blanketing the world in white.
In the stillness, hearts may rush,
Embracing soft, unbroken night.

Footsteps fade in cottoned grace,
Echoes whisper, softly cease.
In the silence, we find our space,
Wrapped in peace, two souls at ease.

Fireside tales and laughs abound,
Warmth ignites against the chill.
In this moment, love is found,
Time stands still, the world stands still.

As daylight fades and stars appear,
We hold each other, dreams alive.
In the quiet, all is clear,
Embracing silence, we will thrive.

Flickering Flames and Chilled Air

Fires crackle, shadows play,
Warmth against the cold night air.
With every flicker, hopes convey,
In the glow, we shed despair.

Outside, the world is wrapped in ice,
Yet here, our hearts ignite the flame.
In every gaze, a sweet entice,
Together, we are not the same.

Cups of cocoa, laughter's cheer,
Moments shared, the time feels right.
In the chill, I hold you near,
Flickering flames through darkest night.

Weaves of warmth in every glance,
Two souls dance in flickering light.
In this embrace, a timeless chance,
Chilled air fades; our love takes flight.

Snug Evenings and Dreamy Visions

In the glow of soft lamplight,
We gather close, hearts alight.
Mugs of warmth in hands we hold,
Whispers of stories yet untold.

Outside the chill winds may blow,
Inside, our laughter starts to flow.
Wrapped in blankets, we drift away,
Creating dreams till break of day.

Laughter Echoes in Dim Light

A flicker of warmth in the air,
Laughter dances without a care.
Faces gleam in the evening glow,
Friends gather round, spirits grow.

Shadows play upon the wall,
Echoing giggles, a joyous call.
Every moment, a treasure found,
In this sweet night where love abounds.

Snowflakes Seep into Memory

Each flake falls soft, a silent kiss,
Reminders of moments wrapped in bliss.
Footprints linger, whispers near,
Memories etched through each snowy sphere.

In a world adorned in white,
Time stands still, a pure delight.
Childhood dreams, they stir and rise,
Snowflakes twirl beneath wintry skies.

The Essence of Winter Whispers

The air is crisp, a gentle sigh,
Nature sleeps beneath the sky.
Frosted branches whisper low,
Secrets only winter knows.

Softly glows the moonlit night,
Casting dreams in silver light.
Cold winds carry tales so grand,
Of winter's touch across the land.

Flurries of Remembrance

Softly fall the flurries,
Whispering tales of yore.
Every flake, a memory,
Drifts on an open shore.

Silent streets hold echoes,
Footprints lost in the gray.
Each place tells a story,
Of times that slipped away.

Frosty breath of winter,
Hides the warmth of the past.
In the stillness, we ponder,
How moments fade so fast.

Yet within the heart's chamber,
Love's glow can never dim.
Flurries swirl and dance,
A timeless, tender hymn.

Twinkling Lights in the Frost

Glimmers in the cold night,
Stars awake in the sky.
Frosted tips of the branches,
Underneath, shadows lie.

Lanterns dot the pathway,
Guiding us through the chill.
Each spark tells a story,
Of warmth, of love, of will.

Twinkling lights surround us,
In this magical place.
They dance like whispers,
In the hush of winter's grace.

With each flicker, a promise,
A reminder to hold tight.
Joy can sparkle softly,
In the calm of the night.

Nostalgia Lingers in the Air

Softly, the memories linger,
Like smoke from a warm fire.
Shadows dance on the walls,
Stirring dreams, a sweet choir.

Whispers of laughter echo,
In the glow of soft lights.
Each sigh brings an old song,
Wrapped in long, gentle nights.

Time bends like a river,
Flowing back to sweet days.
In the air, nostalgia,
In a soft, misty haze.

Capture every moment,
Let each feeling declare,
That love is a treasure,
Nostalgia lingers there.

A Fire's Gentle Story

A fire crackles softly,
Embers glow in the night.
With each flicker and pop,
It tells tales of delight.

Gathered around the warmth,
We share whispers and dreams.
Stories float like shadows,
Glowing as bright as beams.

The flames dance in rhythm,
A ballet of pure grace.
Each spark holds a memory,
In this cozy embrace.

As the night grows deeper,
Hearts open like a door.
In the fire's gentle story,
We find what we adore.

Thoughts Like Snowflakes

Falling softly from the sky,
Each one unique, a fleeting sigh.
Whispers of dreams, they twirl and dance,
In winter's grip, they take their chance.

Glimmers of light in frosty air,
Memories form with utmost care.
Gentle thoughts on chilly nights,
Blanket the world in soft delights.

Patterns weave on cold white ground,
Silent moments, peace is found.
Like snowflakes drift, so do we roam,
In every fall, we find our home.

Catch them quick before they fade,
In their beauty, fears evade.
Thoughts like snowflakes, ever rare,
Each one precious, beyond compare.

Comforts of the Hearth

Glow of fire, the warmth within,
Gentle laughter, where hearts begin.
Surrounded by stories, old and true,
Embers dance, as shadows grew.

Cozy blankets, snug and tight,
In this haven, all feels right.
The crackling wood, a soothing sound,
In this peace, love is found.

Fragrant spices, meals prepared,
Every bite, the soul is bared.
Gathered close, we share our tales,
Through winter storms, our bond prevails.

Comforts linger, soft and bright,
A cherished glow, a guiding light.
In the hearth's heart, we remain,
Together warmed, in joy and pain.

Lanterns in the Night's Embrace

Flickering lights upon the path,
Guiding steps away from wrath.
Hope and dreams in every glow,
Lanterns sway with gentle flow.

Stars above, a woven thread,
Whispers carried where we tread.
Through the dark, their beams invite,
Illuminating hearts in flight.

Faintly shining, tales untold,
In their warmth, we find our gold.
Casting shadows, dances free,
In the night, we learn to see.

Lanterns flicker, words unspoke,
In their light, new journeys woke.
Embrace the night, let worries cease,
In every glow, we find our peace.

The Magic of Stillness

In quiet moments, breath it slow,
Time suspended, tranquil flow.
Nature whispers, secrets bare,
In stillness, find the world laid bare.

Rippling water, a gentle stream,
Reflecting thoughts, a waking dream.
Every pause, a chance to be,
In solitude, we learn to see.

The world outside may rush and race,
But here we find a sacred space.
In every heartbeat, calm we find,
The magic of the still, divine.

Close your eyes, let silence reign,
In the stillness, lose the strain.
For in the hush, our spirits lift,
In timelessness, we find our gift.

Fireside Tales and Fluffy Socks

By the crackling fire we sit,
Wrapped in warmth, each word a gift.
Fluffy socks on chilly toes,
Stories ride the ember's glow.

Shadows dance upon the wall,
Whispers weave through the hall.
Laughter echoes, hearts align,
In this moment, all is fine.

Sipping tea, we share our dreams,
Life is more than it seems.
Fireside tales, oh how they bind,
In cozy wraps, we unwind.

As night deepens, stars appear,
Fueling hopes, dispelling fear.
In our hearts, the glow stays bright,
Fireside tales by soft moonlight.

Cocoa and the Glow of Love

In mugs of cocoa, warmth resides,
Marshmallows melt like love inside.
Each sip shared, a tender glance,
In this moment, hearts do dance.

Outside the world is cold and grey,
Inside we find a brighter day.
Laughter mingles with sweet cream,
In your eyes, I find my dream.

Windows fogged, our breath entwined,
In simple joys, our hearts aligned.
With every sip, my love you'll see,
In cocoa's warmth, it's you and me.

As shadows fade, the fire glows,
In gentle rhythms, our laughter flows.
Cocoa and love, forever bound,
In your embrace, true bliss I've found.

Tranquil Inklings on Snowy Evenings

Snowflakes fall like whispered dreams,
Blanketing the world in gleams.
Tranquil nights, so pure and bright,
In this silence, hearts take flight.

Softly glowing candles sway,
Casting light in soft ballet.
Warmth of blankets, soft and tight,
In this peace, all feels right.

The world outside, a canvas white,
Filling hearts with pure delight.
Inklings of thoughts drift like snow,
Creating magic in the glow.

Moments linger, time stands still,
In gentle winds, we feel the chill.
Snowy evenings, hearts aglow,
In tranquil bliss, our love will flow.

A Symphony of Warmth and Chill

In winter's grasp, the world feels still,
Yet in our hearts, a warmth we instill.
The fire crackles, sweet and bright,
A symphony of warmth through the night.

Outside, the frosty winds do play,
While in our souls, love finds its way.
With every note, a story told,
In harmonies rich, our love unfolds.

Scarves wrapped tight, we venture out,
In laughter bright, we twirl about.
The chill invites a close embrace,
In every heartbeat, a sacred space.

Together we weave this melody,
Of warmth and chill, of you and me.
In every season, come what may,
Our symphony blooms, come night or day.

Tracing Patterns in the Snow

Footprints dance in soft white,
Whispers of the world alight.
Patterns trace a silent tale,
Nature's art, a fleeting veil.

Pine trees sigh beneath the weight,
Snowflakes drift and softly wait.
Each step marks a fleeting dream,
In this quiet, pure regime.

Stars peep through the cloudy haze,
Glistening in the winter's gaze.
Every curve, a fleeting sigh,
In the stillness, beauty lies.

The quiet night begins to glow,
As we walk on through the snow.
Hand in hand, our hearts entwine,
In this peace, we find the divine.

Silent Wishes in a Winter's Breath

Glistening flakes in the moonlight,
Whispers of wishes take flight.
Breath of frost upon the air,
Hope floats softly everywhere.

Branches bend beneath the weight,
Each new snowflake, a small fate.
Silent dreams dance through the night,
Waiting for the morning light.

Laughter echoes, pure and bright,
As we tread through snowy white.
Hearts unite in the still air,
Wishes flutter everywhere.

In the hush, our hopes can swell,
Carried forth on winter's spell.
Each soft breath, a wish we send,
In this moment, hearts will mend.

Evening's Embrace Beneath Stars

The sun dips low, a fiery glow,
As evening paints the world below.
Stars emerge in twilight's grace,
Guiding dreams to a sacred place.

Whispers linger on the breeze,
Carried softly through the trees.
Night unveils a gentle quilt,
Where the heart finds warmth and silt.

In shadows deep, secrets rest,
Moments shared feel like a nest.
Each twinkle tells a story rare,
In evening's hug, we're lost in air.

Together, we face the night,
Finding peace in fading light.
Beneath the stars, our spirits soar,
In this embrace, we crave no more.

Warm Shadows in the Cradle of Night

Flickering flames dance on the wall,
Warm shadows shift, they softly call.
In the cradle of night we find,
A soothing balm for every mind.

The world outside is cold and still,
Yet here, with you, I feel the thrill.
In whispered tones, our secrets spin,
A cozy nook where dreams begin.

The moonlight casts a silver hue,
While stories weave between us two.
Wrapped in warmth, we gently sway,
In this moment, come what may.

Let the night hold us so tight,
As we nestle in its soft light.
In shadows, we find love's embrace,
In the cradle of this true place.

A Tapestry of Stars Above

In the vastness, sparkles glow,
Guiding dreams where stardust flows.
Whispers of night, so calm and deep,
Lullabies for those who sleep.

Each twinkle tells a tale untold,
Of love and loss, both brave and bold.
Beneath this canvas, hearts ignite,
In the embrace of the endless night.

Constellations dance, in cosmic grace,
Time stands still in this sacred space.
A tapestry woven with light and fate,
Inviting souls to celebrate.

Stars above, a shimmering guide,
In their glow, we cannot hide.
They remind us of our place and part,
A map to our dreams, a call to the heart.

Evening's Blanket of Soft White

As day bids farewell, the sky turns grey,
A blanket of softness begins to sway.
Gentle flakes fall, like whispers of peace,
Covering the world, bringing a release.

The trees stand tall, draped in pure white,
A magical scene, a breathtaking sight.
Footsteps crunch on the frosty ground,
In this quiet moment, solace is found.

With every flake, memories blend,
Of warm firesides and time to spend.
The world slows down, wrapped in delight,
As evening descends, soft and bright.

Underneath stars, we now gather close,
To share our stories, to cherish the most.
In evening's embrace, we find our way,
With hearts aglow, come what may.

Chasing Dreams on a Frigid Wind

Through icy gusts, our spirits soar,
Chasing dreams that we can't ignore.
In the chill, hope starts to gleam,
Warming the soul, igniting the dream.

Frosted breaths dance in frozen air,
With each heartbeat, we're stripped bare.
Yet in the cold, our passions ignite,
Guided by stars, we venture into the night.

Whispers of courage call out our name,
In the silence, we play a brave game.
For every challenge, we take a stand,
Hand in hand, we'll make our own land.

On this frigid wind, let us fly,
With dreams ablaze, we'll touch the sky.
No winter's chill can dim our fire,
For in our hearts, beats bright desire.

The Calm After the Fall of Snow

Silence blankets the world outside,
A peaceful hush where dreams reside.
Fresh tracks lead on through pristine white,
In this stillness, the heart takes flight.

Trees wear coats of sparkling frost,
Nature whispers of beauty lost.
The chill in the air, sharp yet sweet,
Every step forward feels like a treat.

Each flake that falls brings joy anew,
Transforming the old into something new.
With a sigh of relief, we breathe it in,
The calm soothes the chaotic din.

As shadows lengthen, the sun's retreat,
The quiet wraps us in warmth complete.
In the snowy embrace, we find our peace,
A moment of grace, where troubles cease.

Whispering Pines and the Celestial Sky

In the forest where secrets dwell,
Winds carry tales too sweet to tell.
Stars above in endless flight,
Guard the dreams of the quiet night.

Branches sway with gentle grace,
Nature's heart in a soft embrace.
Underneath the vast expanse,
Every shadow starts to dance.

Moonbeams lace the darkened ground,
Echoes of silence wrap around.
Pines stand tall, proud, and free,
Whispering hopes to you and me.

Embers glow in the night air,
Moments whispered without a care.
In this realm where whispers sing,
Breathe in peace that forests bring.

A Solitary Candle's Dance

In the stillness of a lonely room,
A candle flickers, casting gloom.
Its flame sways with a silent grace,
Painting shadows on the walls' face.

Each movement tells a tale of light,
Of dreams pursued in the quiet night.
The wax drips down, a slow embrace,
A journey traced in this sacred space.

The fragrance fills the air so sweet,
Capturing whispers of the heartbeat.
In solitude, it shines so bright,
A beacon for the wandering night.

Moments linger in its glow,
Casting warmth in the shadows' flow.
Time stands still, a dance so rare,
In the glow of a candle's care.

Breaths of Warmth in a Frozen Realm

Amidst the snowflakes, soft and light,
Winter breathes in silence bright.
The world is wrapped in a chilly shroud,
Yet warmth resides beneath the cloud.

Footsteps crunch in the frosty air,
Whispers of life linger everywhere.
Crisp and clear, the moments shine,
With every exhale, warmth intertwines.

Branches bow under the weight of snow,
A tapestry where cold winds blow.
Yet in this quiet, hearts remain,
Sparks of joy in winter's reign.

Beneath the surface, life awaits,
In frozen realms where magic creates.
Every breath carries the promise of spring,
In the frozen world, love takes wing.

Drifting Thoughts in the Stillness

In the calm of the evening's grace,
Thoughts drift slowly, finding their place.
Each moment a whisper, a silent song,
Carried on currents where dreams belong.

The stars appear, a glimmering chart,
Mapping the journey of the heart.
In the stillness, truth reveals,
The depth of all that feeling heals.

Time flows gently, a river of night,
Washing over with soft, golden light.
Every heartbeat, a rhythm deep,
Guiding the thoughts that gently sweep.

As shadows gather and daylight fades,
Drifting thoughts become serenades.
In the stillness, we find our way,
A tapestry woven with night and day.

Echoes of Laughter by the Firelight

Flames dance in the night,
Whispers of joy take flight.
Friends gather round so near,
As laughter fills the air.

Stories shared with delight,
Memories shining bright.
The warmth wraps like a cloak,
In the fire's gentle smoke.

Crackling embers glow red,
Each word a thread well-spread.
We weave our tales so fine,
In this moment, divine.

Time slips in soft repose,
While the night graciously glows.
Echoes of laughter ring,
In the heart, forever sing.

The Magic of Midwinter's Embrace

Snowflakes fall like dreams,
Blanketing the quiet streams.
Nights adorned in silver lace,
Winter's beauty, a soft grace.

Fires crackle, shadows play,
Beneath the stars, we sway.
Embers warm our cheeks so fair,
In this spell, we breathe the air.

Hot cocoa swirls in hand,
With each sip, we understand.
The magic in this chill,
Bound around with winter's will.

A tranquil hush surrounds,
In this peace, content abounds.
Midwinter's embrace so true,
Wraps us whole, me and you.

Telling Tales Beneath the Hushed Stars

Under the blanket of night,
Stars whisper secrets, so bright.
Stories gather like the dew,
In the stillness, old and new.

Fables of courage and grace,
Each tale finds its rightful place.
With eyes wide in wonder shared,
Beneath the cosmos, hearts bared.

The moon a witness, aglow,
As gentle winds begin to blow.
In this space, our souls connect,
With every word, a deep respect.

Dreams take flight in starlit skies,
Each tale a spark that never dies.
Telling tales, hand in hand,
Guided by the night's soft band.

A Symphony of Shadows and Warmth

In the dusk, shadows blend,
Warmth wraps us, a faithful friend.
The twilight hums a low tune,
As day surrenders to the moon.

Crickets sing their soft refrain,
While the world hums with a vein.
Each heartbeat syncs with the light,
Creating a symphony of night.

Flickering candles, shadows dance,
A moment held in quiet chance.
Where laughter echoes, love ignites,
In the embracing folds of nights.

Together we find our core,
In whispers, we ask for more.
A symphony, both rich and deep,
In shadows and warmth, we find sleep.

Gentle Warmth of Home

In the corner a fire glows,
Whispers of comfort in the air.
Fingers wrapped around warm mugs,
Laughter dances without a care.

Walls adorned with love's embrace,
Memories linger in every nook.
Soft blankets pile on the couch,
A safe haven, a cherished book.

The smell of bread, fresh and warm,
Echoes of joy fill the halls.
Families gather, hearts transform,
In every heart, a love that calls.

Evening settles, stars appear,
Quiet moments, stories told.
In the gentle warmth, we hold dear,
Home's embrace, a treasure of gold.

Picturesque Frost in Soft Light

Morning breaks with a silken sheen,
Frosted branches like diamonds shine.
Nature's canvas, a pure scene,
In soft light, the world aligns.

Breath of winter in every ray,
Footprints softly crunch the ground.
Colors muted, yet they play,
In this magic, peace is found.

Icicles hang like whispered dreams,
Curtains of ice, all aglow.
Nature's breath in sparkling beams,
A fleeting beauty, a gentle show.

Soon the warmth will softly creep,
But for now, let the stillness reign,
In this moment, memories keep,
Wrapped in frost, forever remain.

The Sound of Softness

Gentle whispers of the night,
Crickets sing a tender tune.
Rustling leaves, the moon's soft light,
Nature sways in a sweet swoon.

Raindrops fall like quiet sighs,
Pillow clouds, their weightless grace.
In the dark, the spirit flies,
Finding peace in this embrace.

Pages turning, stories blend,
The soft crackle of a flame.
In every heartbeat, nights descend,
The sound of softness calls our name.

Time slows down in twilight hours,
Wrapped in warmth, we softly dream.
In every moment, love empowers,
A gentle stream, a flowing theme.

Quietude Wrapped in Layers

In the stillness, silence speaks,
Wrapped in blankets, layers deep.
A sanctuary for the weak,
In quietude, our souls shall leap.

Snowflakes dance as shadows pass,
Whispers of a hidden grace.
Each soft touch, a fleeting glass,
Moments held in time and space.

Candlelight flickers, shadows play,
Stories woven in golden thread.
In this cocoon, we must stay,
Finding solace, love's soft bed.

As night descends, we close our eyes,
Dreams take flight in tranquil streams.
Wrapped in layers, love never dies,
In quietude, we weave our dreams.

Serenade of the Frosty Breeze

The frost whispers low, under moon's soft glow,
A dance of icy notes, where tranquil rivers flow.
Each breath forms a mist, in the chill of the night,
The world wrapped in dreams, bathed in silver light.

The branches they sway, in a delicate waltz,
The stars sparkle bright, as if none were at fault.
The chilly embrace, cradles hearts with ease,
In this silent serenade, sung by the breeze.

With every soft sigh, the night holds its breath,
A melody drifts, whispering tales of death.
Yet life finds a way, in each fragile freeze,
Awakening warmth, in the grip of the breeze.

Flickers in the Stillness

In shadows they gleam, where silence takes flight,
Flickers of hope, in the cloak of the night.
A gentle reminder, through the dark we weave,
The whispers of dreams, in the hearts that believe.

Stars tremble with grace, above quiet streams,
Reflecting the stories, of lost, distant dreams.
They shimmer like fire, in the blanket of sky,
Each spark tells a secret, of moments gone by.

As night wraps around, in its delicate throng,
The mind sings a lullaby, soft and long.
Flickers in stillness, a vision unfolds,
Painting the heavens in glimmers of gold.

Blanketed by Silence

A hush descends softly, like snow on the ground,
Blanketed whispers, where no echoes are found.
The world takes a pause, in the stillness we lie,
Wrapped tight in the quiet, beneath the vast sky.

Each heartbeat resounds, in the echoing peace,
A refuge from chaos, where worries release.
The air wears a shroud, of calm and of grace,
In this tranquil moment, we find our own space.

No battles to fight, just the warmth that we seek,
In silence, we gather, hear the heart speak.
Life slows its relentless, frantic-paced dance,
In the beauty of quiet, we take a soft chance.

Heartbeats in the Quiet

The night wraps around, cradling all souls near,
Heartbeats in the quiet, everything feels clear.
Underneath the stars, life pulses with grace,
In moments of stillness, we all find our place.

The world fades away, like the echo of time,
In the warmth of your gaze, I find rhythm and rhyme.
We share this soft pulse, in the hush of the dark,
A symphony of feelings, igniting the spark.

With every soft thrum, connections ignite,
In this space we hold, everything feels right.
Heartbeats in the quiet, a timeless embrace,
Where love writes its story, in the stillness of space.

The Nostalgic Melody of Crackling Wood

In the hearth, the embers glow,
Whispers dance in firelight's flow.
Each crackle tells a tale anew,
Of seasons past and skies so blue.

Wooden warmth fills the chilly air,
Memory's echo, a tender snare.
With every pop, a heartbeat feels,
The nostalgia of enchanted reels.

Flickering shadows paint the room,
As night unfolds its velvet gloom.
Wrapped in blankets, stories weave,
In crackling wood, we dare believe.

Fireside dreams take to the night,
In glow so soft, our souls ignite.
Each moment cherished, never fade,
In wood's embrace, our hearts are laid.

Starlit Dreams in Woolen Layers

Underneath the vast night sky,
Woolen layers wrapped up high.
In dreams, beneath the starlit sheen,
Whispers soft, and visions keen.

Galaxies in twinkle's light,
Bring comfort through the chilly night.
Each star a wish, a hope, a kiss,
In woolen folds, distilled bliss.

Crickets sing their ancient song,
In harmony, we all belong.
Nestled close, through shadows swayed,
In dreams of starlight, love displayed.

Woolen layers, warm embrace,
With the universe, we interlace.
Beneath the stars, our spirits soar,
In dreams woven, forevermore.

Hibernation of the Heart

In winter's chill, the heart finds rest,
Wrapped in silence, nature's vest.
Beneath the frost, a pulse so slow,
In solitude, emotions grow.

Each flake that falls, a gentle sigh,
Whispers in the moonlit sky.
Dreams tucked away, like seeds concealed,
Awaiting spring, their fate revealed.

Time to pause, to breathe, to mend,
As frozen streams begin to bend.
Through icy veils, a fire glows,
In hibernation, love still flows.

The heart knows when to bide its time,
In stillness, there's a quiet rhyme.
From echoes deep, new warmth will start,
This winter leads to spring's sweet heart.

Stories Shared in the Glow

Gathered close around the fire,
Hearts ignite with whispered desire.
In the glow, the tales take flight,
Stories spun through the velvet night.

Each voice a thread, a memory bright,
Weaving laughter, sorrow, delight.
Through flickered flames, our spirits blend,
As time slows down, the hours suspend.

Elders share their wisdom's grace,
While children dream of distant places.
In shared tales, the world expands,
Uniting lofty hopes and hands.

Beneath the stars, our hearts entwine,
In every word, a sacred sign.
In the glow of fire, we reside,
Bonded forever, side by side.

Shadows Dance on the Windowpane

Shadows flicker, soft and light,
As twilight whispers, day to night.
Figures sway in gentle grace,
Framed by time's enchanting space.

Silent stories, secrets weave,
In the stillness, we believe.
Ghostly figures, fleeting glance,
In the darkness, shadows dance.

The Gentle Embrace of a Crystal Night

Under stars that softly glow,
Moonlight blankets all below.
Whispers travel on the breeze,
Through the branches, past the trees.

Each twinkle tells of dreams so bright,
In the stillness of the night.
Crystals spark in skies so vast,
Moments cherished, never past.

Hearthside Memories in the Glow

Crackling embers fill the air,
Warmth and laughter linger there.
Stories share on winter's eve,
In the hearth, we weave, believe.

Flickering light paints the walls,
Echoes of our childhood calls.
Every smile, a cherished trace,
In these moments, we find grace.

Where Snowflakes Whisper Secrets

Snowflakes fall, a silent song,
In their dance, they all belong.
Whispers carried, soft and light,
Nature's blanket, pure and white.

Each unique, a fleeting sight,
Frosty kisses, pure delight.
Embracing earth, a soft caress,
In their presence, we find rest.

Winter's Tender Embrace

Whispers of snow fall soft and light,
Blanketing earth in purest white.
Trees stand quiet, branches bare,
In winter's chill, a calm we share.

The moon reflects on glistening frost,
In this stillness, we find what's lost.
With every breath, the air feels clear,
In winter's hold, we draw near.

The fires crackle, warmth inside,
As we gather, hearts open wide.
Through frosted windows, the world glows,
Wrapped in winter's soft repose.

A season's gift, both harsh and sweet,
In the cold, our souls meet.
In tender ways, it pulls us close,
Winter's touch feels like a dose.

A Cup of Serenity

Steam rises from the porcelain cup,
A moment's peace, we lift it up.
With every sip, the world slows down,
In simplicity, we wear a crown.

The warmth flows gently, a soothing balm,
In its embrace, we find our calm.
Notes of spice dancing in the air,
In this quiet, we feel rare.

Outside, life rushes, wild and fast,
But here, we cherish each moment passed.
The swirl of flavors, so divine,
In this cup, our hearts entwine.

We breathe in deeply, lost in thought,
In warmth of tea, the battles fought.
A cup of serenity, small yet grand,
In its depths, we understand.

Frost's Gentle Caress on Warmth

In morning light, a glimmer shines,
Frost on leaves, like silver lines.
Nature's art, a fleeting show,
Frosty kisses as winds blow.

Each blade awakens, crisp and bright,
Dew drops linger in soft light.
While the sun rises, warmth will fight,
But frosts hold on with all their might.

The chill retreats, but memories stay,
Of frosted whispers at break of day.
A dance of seasons, cold and warm,
Together they weave, a world to charm.

In fleeting moments, beauty lies,
Frost's gentle touch, a sweet surprise.
As warmth prevails, the frost will yield,
But in our hearts, its grace is sealed.

Beneath the Weight of Snow

Blankets of white drape the earth,
Each flake a promise, a new birth.
Silent moments, nature's hush,
Under the weight, we feel the rush.

Paths concealed, familiar sight,
In winter's beauty, we find our light.
Footprints lead through drifts so deep,
In snowy realms, our dreams can leap.

Branches bow under winter's load,
Yet in stillness, a new story's flowed.
Crisp air fills our lungs, we embrace,
In winter's arms, we find our place.

As seasons change, we will recall,
Beneath the weight, we rise, we fall.
Nature's cycle, a timeless dance,
In snow's embrace, we take our chance.

Soundtrack of Soft Sighs

In whispers soft, the echoes play,
A melody of dreams that sway.
Each breath a note, each heart a chord,
In silence spoken, love's reward.

The gentle breeze, it weaves around,
A lullaby in every sound.
With every sigh, a story told,
In harmony, our hearts unfold.

The twilight sky begins to glow,
As shadows dance in fading flow.
With every breath, we find our place,
In softest sighs, we embrace grace.

So let the night wrap us in dreams,
Where starlight falls and silence beams.
Together here, our hearts will soar,
In the soundtrack of love, forevermore.

The Beauty of Winter's Whisper

In winter's hush, the world is still,
A canvas white, a gentle thrill.
Snowflakes fall like whispers pure,
In silence, find the heart's allure.

Frosty breaths upon the glass,
Nature's art in moments pass.
The trees adorned in crystal lace,
A beauty found in quiet grace.

The air is crisp, it bites and plays,
In chilly light of waning days.
Yet warmth within our spirits rise,
For love's the fire, the sweetest prize.

Embrace the chill, the frost, the night,
For in the dark, our souls take flight.
The beauty of the winter's hum,
A serenade of peace, we come.

Snowbound Silhouettes

Through blizzards fierce, the shadows roam,
In snowbound fields, we find our home.
Silhouettes dance in twilight's hue,
As winter whispers, soft and true.

The moonlight casts a silver glow,
On frosty paths where dreamers go.
Each step we take, a story's spun,
In winter's arms, we become one.

With every flake, a chance to dream,
In chilly nights, our hearts will beam.
The quiet grace of frozen nights,
Brings warmth within, our souls ignites.

So hand in hand, let's face the chill,
In snowbound love, our hearts will thrill.
Together we embrace the night,
In softest hugs, our spirits light.

Evening Light in Chilly Air

As daylight fades, the colors gleam,
In evening light, we start to dream.
The air is crisp, a cooling sigh,
Beneath the vast and twilight sky.

Stars emerge like tiny flames,
In chilly winds, they call our names.
With every glance, the world transforms,
In magic spun from winter's norms.

The shadows lengthen, quietly creep,
As nature sighs, the night, it keeps.
In warmth we find a soft embrace,
In evening's light, we trace each face.

The chill surrounds, yet hearts feel warm,
In love's embrace, we find our charm.
So here we stand, beneath the skies,
Together lost in evening's sighs.

Fireside Fortunes and Flickering Fancies

The flames dance in a warm embrace,
As stories mix with smoke's sweet trace.
Fortunes whispered in the night,
Flickering shadows, a wondrous sight.

Dreams ignite with each soft spark,
Hopes like embers, glowing in the dark.
Moments shared, hearts intertwine,
In this cozy nook, all feels divine.

The crackle sings a siren's song,
As laughter fills the air so strong.
Together we weave, our fate, our cheer,
In these fireside fortunes, love is clear.

As flickering fancies dance and sway,
We hold this warmth, come what may.
Each gentle whisper, every glance,
In this sacred space, we take our chance.

The Heart's Cradle on Glistening Nights

Underneath the silver moon,
With stars that twinkle, soft as June.
The heart's cradle gently rocks,
A lullaby that time unlocks.

Whispers drift on the midnight air,
Promises made without a care.
Every heartbeat sings a song,
In this cradle where we belong.

Glistening nights, so pure and bright,
A haven wrapped in a dreamer's light.
Hand in hand, we face the dawn,
In this embrace, worries are gone.

Each moment cherished, love's own flight,
Together we soar through the starlit night.
In the heart's cradle, our dreams alight,
Guided by hope, we chase the light.

Glows of Hope in Winter's Grip

In winter's grasp, the world is white,
Yet glows of hope ignite the night.
With frosty breath, we share our dreams,
In the chill, warmth softly gleams.

Bundled tight, we walk the path,
Laughter echoes, warmth from the hearth.
Each step we take, a promise made,
In the snow, our fears will fade.

The chill can't dim the love we hold,
As stories of courage dare be told.
Together we rise, against the frost,
In glows of hope, we count the cost.

We find our way through winter's clutch,
With every heartbeat, we feel the touch.
Hope lights the way through the darkest night,
In such moments, we find our might.

Constellations in a Frosty Sky

Above the earth, where silence reigns,
Constellations paint the sky in chains.
Each star a story, bold and bright,
In the frosty air, they take flight.

Beneath this dome, we search each name,
In whispers soft as winter's flame.
Guiding us with their ancient spark,
In the dark, we leave our mark.

Together we weave our wishes high,
With dreams that span the endless sky.
In the frosted night, hearts align,
In constellations, our love will shine.

With every glance, new paths unfold,
Adventures written in stories bold.
In this winter's night, forever we fly,
Chasing the stars in a frosty sky.

Milton Keynes UK
Ingram Content Group UK Ltd.
UKHW022144111124
451073UK00007B/186